Buckin

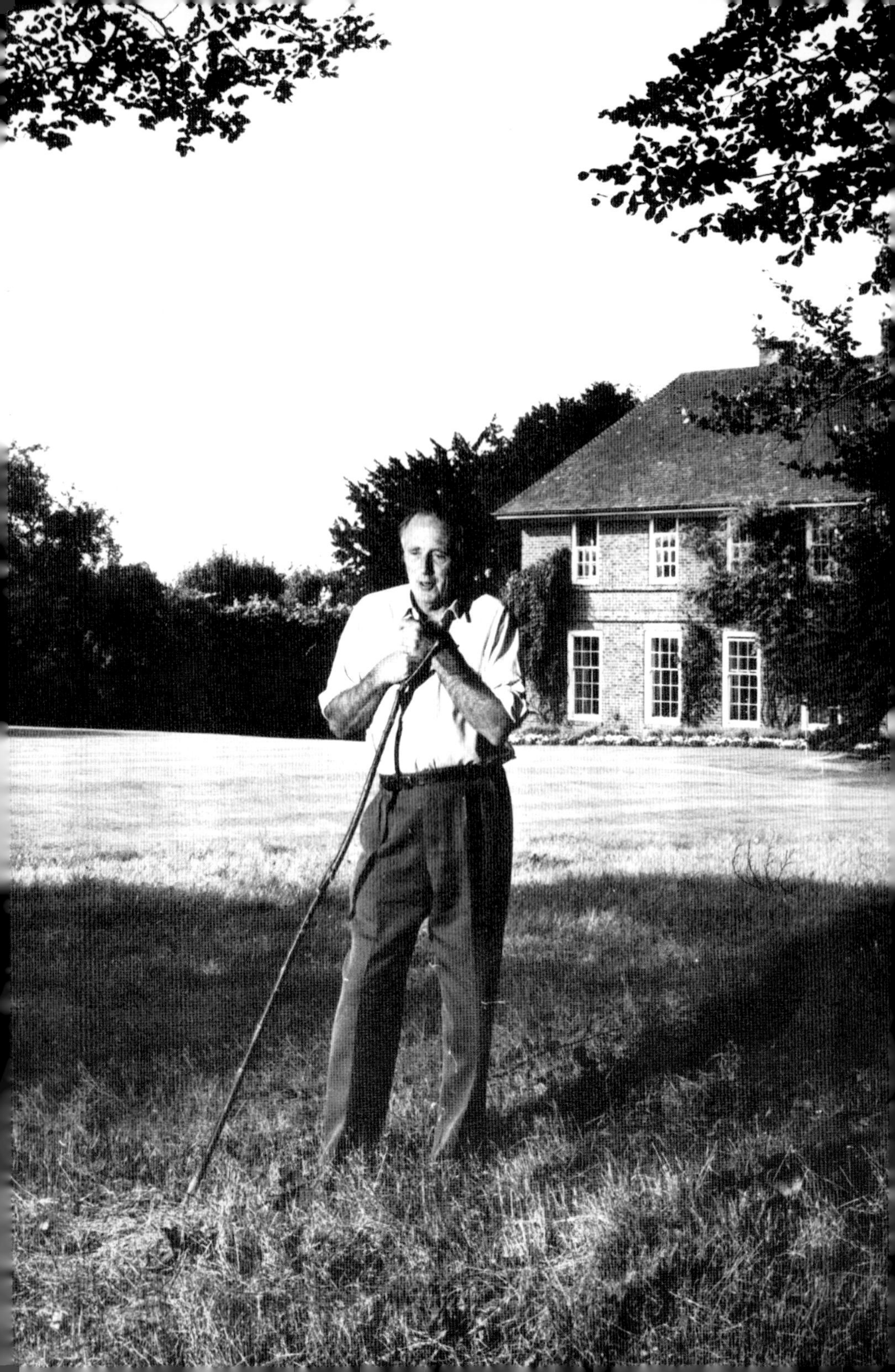

Alastair Fairley

Bucking the Trend

The life and times of the ninth
Earl De La Warr 1900–1976

with a foreword by
Marco Goldschmied
President of the Royal Institute of
British Architects

The Pavilion Trust

Bucking the Trend:
The life and times of the ninth Earl De La Warr
Copyright © Alastair Fairley 2001

First published 2001 by
The Pavilion Trust
De La Warr Pavilion
Marina
Bexhill on Sea
TN40 1DP

ISBN 0 9540350 0 3

Designed by Jeremy Brook, Graphic Ideas
Printed by Hastings Printing Company

Front cover: Ninth Earl De La Warr, Postmaster General, 1953
Back cover: De La Warr Pavilion, 1998. Photograph: John Riddy
Frontispiece: Ninth Earl De La Warr at Fishersgate, 1970
Photographs on pages 14, 17, 21, 23, 37, 39, 61 courtesy of Bexhill Museum

Contents

Foreword	6
Acknowledgements	7
Bucking the Trend	9
A part of history	11
Buckhurst, Bexhill and the Brasseys	15
The rise to influence	27
Britain in the 1930s:	
The rise of Modernism	30
The De La Warr Pavilion	33
A hand in history	43
De La Warr's war	47
Back in the fold	55
Safeguarding the future	62
References	64

Foreword

The Royal Institute of British Architects has had to wage many battles since its foundation in 1834. In the 1930s, one fight the RIBA took on was the question of foreign architects arriving in Britain in their bid to escape Nazi persecution. 'At a time when so many of our young and vital architects are in a desperate position', protested the *Fascist Week* in 1934, 'the Royal Institute of British Architects chooses to welcome alien architects and to encourage them in professional practice within this country'. Can you imagine if the RIBA had not fought to allow emigré architects such as Erich Mendelsohn, one of the joint designers of the De La Warr Pavilion, to work alongside their British counterparts? Both humanity and architecture would have suffered.

Encouraging the highest standard of architectural integrity has always been one of the RIBA's aims. It was the RIBA, for example, that worked alongside the ninth Earl De La Warr, in assessing the competition that led to the design of the Bexhill-on-Sea building. But the RIBA is also the memory of the architectural past, maintained through its famous Library to which, in 1955, Mendelsohn's widow presented three precious sketch designs that her husband had made of the De La Warr Pavilion. Each drawing is a small tour-de-force of design and draughtsmanship, reflective of that great seaside building, a masterpiece of 20th century architecture, which thankfully still stands proudly today as the ninth Earl's living memorial.

Marco Goldschmied
RIBA President

Acknowledgements

Alastair Fairley is most grateful to the many people who have helped him compile this biography and found the time to read, edit and provide information for the finished text.

Much of the original research and interviewing for the background material was undertaken by Jill Theis, without whose enthusiasm this book would not have been written. Jill is a founder member of the Pavilion Trust, Friends of the De La Warr Pavilion. She was a Rother District Councillor between 1983–99 and lives near Bexhill in the village of Catsfield, site of the Normanhurst Estate, the birthplace of the ninth Earl De La Warr.

I would like to extend my thanks to: The Earl and Countess De La Warr; Frank and Lady Kitty Giles; Sir John Smith CH CBE; Alan Powers of the Twentieth Century Society; Chris Whittick, Senior Archivist, East Sussex Records Office and Julian Porter, Curator, Bexhill Museum. I would also like to thank Mabel Derry; Birkin Haward; Tom Hammick; Margaret Jones; Peter Kirby; Suzanne Leonard; Heather Morrey; Anne Rowley, Bexhill Library; Graham Whitham and Jan Wicks, Chairman of the Pavilion Trust.

The Pavilion Trust are most grateful for the kind assistance of the following sponsors who have contributed towards the cost of this publication: The Manifold Trust, The Pilgrim Trust, The Rayne Foundation and Bexhill Museum.

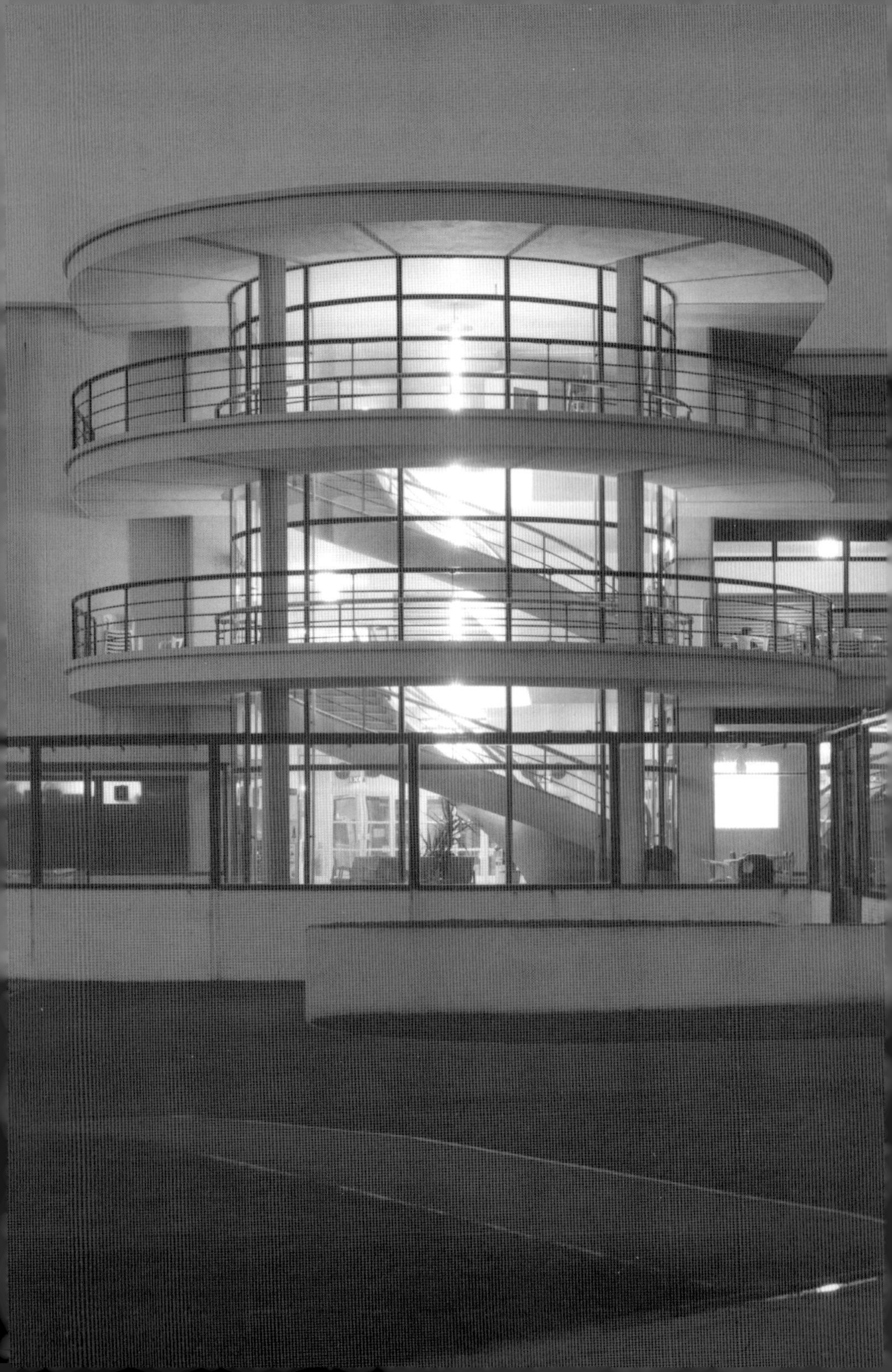

Bucking the Trend

In a country seeking to limit the influence of hereditary peers, there is a certain irony that so many of the lasting landmarks which contribute to making Britain 'Great' have been the result of the vision, foresight and often patronage of our most able aristocrats.

Of the many achievements of Herbrand Edward Dundonald Brassey Sackville, the ninth Earl De La Warr, none is more visible than the pioneering De La Warr Pavilion in Bexhill, an acknowledged world-class building and one of the finest examples of twentieth-century modernist architecture world-wide still open to the public.

With its strong, clean lines and extensive use of glass, concrete and steel, the De La Warr Pavilion is striking even today. When it was built in 1935, its style and use of materials was truly extraordinary, in stark contrast to the genteel, late Victorian and Edwardian architecture surrounding it with which Bexhill had become so familiar.

That such a controversial, bold building could have been built at all is due, almost entirely, to the vision, tenacity and ideals of one man – the ninth Earl De La Warr. As Mayor of Bexhill it was he who instigated the plan to create an entertainment palace by the sea; he who backed the plans to find a modernist solution to the building's design; he who balanced the twin roles of civic leader and courtly aristocrat to make the Pavilion a shining example of Socialist achievement, a seaside palace designed to bring the pleasures of culture, health and relaxation – formerly the privileges of only the wealthy – to the wider public.

◀ De La Warr Pavilion, 1998. Photograph: John Riddy

For many, the idea may seem perverse that an aristocrat – and a wealthy one – should break the mould, challenge convention and work tirelessly for the interests of the ordinary man or woman. But the ninth Earl was no ordinary aristocrat. Indeed, as the knowledge grows of his family's background, his ancestry and his upbringing, the term 'pioneer' crops up with startling regularity. On final examination, it would have been all the more strange had 'Buck' De La Warr, as he was known all his life, *not* been out of the ordinary and *not* gone on to make his own distinctive mark on the twentieth century.

A part of history

The story of the De La Warr Pavilion and its founder starts not in the heady, confident days between two World Wars, but deep in the mediaeval history of England.

The De La Warr title is an ancient one, created when Edward I made Roger La Warr a baron in 1299. But like many of the oldest families in England, many more titles, land and rights were to be acquired over the coming centuries. The barony passed, through marriage, to the third Baron West in 1426. The new Baron De La Warr had also, by then, acquired another name still living in today's peerage – Cantelupe – after his father had married the daughter and heir to Sir John Cantelupe.

No titled family spanning 700 years can be entirely free from treachery, and the De La Warrs are no different. In the mid-sixteenth century Thomas West, the tenth Baron, adopted his nephew, William West, as his heir, having no sons of his own to whom he could pass on the title. He was to rue the day for, soon after, William attempted to poison his uncle, albeit unsuccessfully. The plot discovered, William was promptly disinherited and, with the tenth Baron's death in 1554, both the Baronies of West and De La Warr fell into abeyance.

Had the times been different, the titles could have disappeared altogether. But with the Northern Rebellion raging, led by the disillusioned Catholic Earls of Northumberland and Westmorland, opportunities for royal favour abounded. Redeeming himself in battle, William West was re-ennobled by Elizabeth I, the queen appointing him first Baron De La Warr in the second creation of the title in 1572. Coincidentally, this was just two years after another family ultimately to be linked with the De La Warr title – the Sackvilles – had been granted the Manor of Bexhill.

Like the ninth Earl's own family, Buck's ancestors also travelled greatly, too. Few were more pioneering than Thomas West, the third Baron De La Warr, whose dramatic arrival in Jamestown, on America's Eastern coastline, in 1610 brought vital food and supplies to the early colonists, changing the face of America for ever.

Some ten years before the Mayflower set sail with the Pilgrim Fathers, only 150 starving colonists had survived of the 900 original adventurers who had colonised Jamestown. Despairing, the colonists set sail down the James river for England, abandoning the colony, only to encounter De La Warr and his vital supply ships at Mulberry Island the very next day. After a good feasting, the colonists returned to Jamestown three days later.[1]

The third Baron's arrival is seen by many as a turning point in the colonisation of America. He was to serve as Governor of the new Royal Colony of Virginia for almost a year until his departure for England in March 1611. But his name lives on in American history. Just months after De La Warr's arrival one of his captains, Samuel Argall, was blown off course in a storm while exploring the coast, finding refuge in a strange bay. Rescued once more, Argall appropriately named the bay after his Governor. The state of Delaware was born.

It is doubtful that Baron De La Warr ever saw or explored the bay, river and state which now bears his name. Three months after his arrival in June, the colonists attacked and vanquished the local

Paspagegh Indians. The uneasy truce which followed allowed the pioneers to settle down over the next fifteen years to the cultivation of tobacco – an occupation the Baron's twentieth century descendant was to continue. By 1625, the colony of Virginia was firmly established under Royal Charter and had over 1000 people living in it.[2] England, courtesy of Baron De La Warr, was getting rich from the profits.

The De La Warrs continued to play an important role in England's involvement in America. General John West, for example, was Governor of New York during the mid-eighteenth century, the role earning him an earldom in 1761 and bestowing upon him the title of Viscount Cantelupe, the name brought to the family over 300 years earlier.

But it is not until the nineteenth century that the De La Warr name starts to be associated with Bexhill, and then only through marriage of George West, the fifth Earl, to Lady Elizabeth Sackville in 1813.

Mary and Elizabeth Sackville were the only surviving children of John Sackville, the third Duke of Dorset. On his death the dukedom had passed to his son Frederick who died soon after, at only 21, unmarried. The dukedom then passed to a cousin, Charles, the fifth Duke, who also died without an heir, leaving the dukedom extinct. With a shortage of male heirs, the estates passed on down the female line of the family, but Mary was to die before her sister Elizabeth. Thus the duchy's estates of Knole, Buckhurst and Bexhill passed to Elizabeth and, through her, to her new family of De La Warr.

The De La Warrs merged the Sackville name with their own, becoming Sackville-Wests, only to drop the latter part of the name later that century, the seventh Earl and his family being known simply as Sackville. This is perhaps odd, given that it was the name of West, rather than their newly-adopted name, with which the Barons De La Warr had been associated for some 600 years.

However, like De La Warr, the Sackville-West name is also famous in British history. Vita Sackville-West, the renowned writer and gardener, was the fifth Earl De La Warr's great-granddaughter, and born at Knole in 1892. She married the politician and diarist Sir Harold Nicolson, who often was to work alongside her equally prominent cousin, Earl De La Warr, in and out of Government office. She is buried alongside Buck in the family chapel at Withyham, Sussex.

The Earl De La Warr coat of arms

Buckhurst, Bexhill and the Brasseys

His family steeped in history, the ninth Earl had many great ancestors to look to when making his own mark on the world. But it was more recent influences, from both his father's and mother's remarkable families, which shaped Buck's career.

With its estates of Bexhill and Buckhurst, the De La Warr estates were vast. By the late 1880s the family owned over 17,000 acres, including large swathes of the Ashdown Forest and considerable land, properties and valuable sea frontage in Bexhill itself. However, as the slump in agriculture took hold, the seventh Earl – Buck's grandfather – started to plough money into the development of Bexhill as a fashionable seaside resort with high quality entertainment and a reputation for its health-giving environment.

In 1883 he constructed the sea wall, enabling elegant parades of housing and shops to be built, and added 'on-Sea' to Bexhill's name. It was a clear message that the resort, with its new railway link to London, was moving forward. It was also a message both his son and grandson – the ninth Earl – were to repeat, with even greater success.

But despite the seventh Earl's investment, the town's very development was to establish a division in Bexhill townsfolk, traces of which can still be seen in the debate over the future of Bexhill even today.

With much of his family's fortune tied up in land, the seventh Earl paid for much of his investment in Bexhill in kind, giving a large portion of the land on the town's seafront to John Webb, his building contractor, in part-payment for his work. The division it created – between the commercial trading area of the town based on Webb's land and the high class housing, hotels and entertainment venues on De La Warr's – was to simmer for decades, boiling over spectacularly even fifty years later, when the ninth Earl proposed the building of the De La Warr Pavilion itself.

The issue went beyond differences between tradesmen and the upper part of Bexhill society – or snobbery, in other words. More, it was a division between those dependent on tourism, and those of more independent means who found visitors to the resort an intrusion and who were reluctant to pay for the facilities they required. Throughout, the issue has centred on local rates, one side of the division reluctant to pay for facilities which were, largely, located in the other side's land. And, as Bexhill grew, the division was to become even more distinct.

In 1892 the seventh Earl passed the administration of his estate in Bexhill entirely to his son, the flamboyant Viscount Cantelupe who, with his equally remarkable wife, Muriel, set about creating what many now see as Bexhill's 'golden age', a period which saw much of the town's development as a high-class Victorian and Edwardian resort.

All the main hotels were built in the period – the Granville and later the Metropole being the grandest – two golf clubs were constructed, the Earl also building the Kursaal pavilion in 1896 to provide entertainment for the resort.

By then, Lord Cantelupe had succeeded his father as the new eighth Earl and, clearly, held Bexhill in the palm of his hand. Elected

Viscount and Viscountess Cantelupe, 1895

Buckhurst Park, 1902

chairman of the new Urban Council, he negotiated licenses to bring electricity to the town, being already director of the town's water and gas companies. Few, it appeared could – or indeed wanted to – stand in the way of his and his wife's vision for the resort. And the vision was that of a pioneer.

For example, in 1895, the town was to become the first in the country to permit mixed bathing. In 1898, the Kursaal became the first place in Bexhill to show motion pictures, albeit a velograph of Gladstone's funeral, but ground-breaking nevertheless. A cycle track was also laid along the East Parade, and international cycling tournaments were held at the De La Warr home, The Manor House, attended by nobility and royalty including, at one tournament in 1897, Grand Duke Michael of Russia.

The eighth Earl was also clearly as fascinated with four wheels as he was with two. Chairman of the Dunlop tyre company since 1897, he wasted no time bringing the new sport of motor racing to Bexhill – and Britain – after visiting the 1901 Nice motor races. One year later, the town was to hold the country's first-ever international motor race and speed trials, starting a tradition in the town which continues to this day.

But all was not so happy at home. By the late 1890s the eighth Earl had met and taken as mistress an actress from the Kursaal music hall. His lavish spending saw him sell large tracts of the De La Warr estates to pay his mounting bills. In 1898, business failure nearly bankrupted him, and in 1899 he left the country to cover the Boer War as a correspondent for *The Globe* newspaper. The marriage never recovered and Buck's mother and father split in 1902 in a rather public – and certainly scandalous for the period – divorce.

It is not known how much the young Buck had to do with his father after his parents' divorce. On his return, wounded, from the war, the eighth Earl briefly became Mayor of Bexhill, in 1903. The same year he also remarried, although he was not to wed Miss Turner, the actress cited in the proceedings, but a new *amour*, Hilda Clavering. While this marriage lasted longer than his previous one, its end came in a similar fashion, the Earl being divorced in 1914 by his wife on the grounds of adultery and desertion. A year later he was dead, succumbing to rheumatic fever in Messina, Sicily, while en route to the Dardanelles campaign of World War I. He was only 46.

Clearly, both in his life and in his untimely death, the eighth Earl had a major impact on his son, the young Lord Buckhurst. As the inheritor of the much reduced family estates, Buck was to continue his family's influence on the character, buildings and life of Bexhill. He was still only a boy of fifteen, at school at Eton, when he became the ninth Earl De La Warr. Power and influence had been thrust upon him at a young age. Without doubt, it was an experience which was to prepare him well for future years, for it was repeated often.

While title, position and ancestry may have brought certain duties to the young Earl, it is the influence of Buck's mother, Muriel, which many see as the foundation for his approach to carrying them out. And it is in that approach – whether to civic duty, public office, social progress or life in general – that the ninth Earl De La Warr has matched, and perhaps even outshone, his pioneering ancestors.

Knights, explorers, allies of Kings and Queens – over the centuries the De La Warrs could count them all. The ninth Earl's family from his mother's side were pioneers too, although of an altogether more modern kind.

Muriel Brassey came from a hugely successful, but rather unconventional family. Her grandfather, Thomas Brassey, was a famous railway contractor. By the time he died in 1870, he had already built one twentieth of the world's railway lines, bringing the family enormous wealth and influence.

By the age of only 32, her father (also Thomas) had become MP for Hastings, and was raised first to a Baron, in 1886, and then an Earl in King George V's Coronation honours of 1911. His distinguished career was particularly concerned with naval affairs. He was Secretary and Civil Lord of the Admiralty and Governor of Victoria from 1895-1900. He wrote a major work on British naval history and founded the yearbook *Brassey's Annual*, a major defence annual still published to this day.

Thomas Brassey was also a notable benefactor to both the towns of Hastings and neighbouring Bexhill, where he was to be elected Mayor in 1907. In an act strangely foreshadowing his grandson's role with Bexhill's Pavilion, he presented the Brassey Institute to Hastings in 1879 "to provide for the intellectual and artistic development among the inhabitants". The Institute comprised a museum, classrooms and a library.

Muriel's mother was just as remarkable, if not more so, given the position of women of the day. One of the first pioneering women travellers, Annie Brassey sailed the world's oceans in the family's yacht, *The Sunbeam*. The voyage in 1876-77 was the first-ever circumnavigation of the globe by steam yacht and her book, *A Voyage in the Sunbeam*, became a best-seller translated into seventeen different languages. Her unique collection of artifacts from her voyages, now forms the major part of both Hastings and

Annie Brassey and her daughters collecting marine specimens in the Caribbean, c1885

Thomas and Annie Brassey

Bexhill Museum's collections. Tragically, she died of malaria aboard *The Sunbeam* while en route to Mauritius in 1887 and was buried at sea. She was only 48.

Muriel's younger sister Marie was also to rise to influence, marrying Freeman Thomas, the future Marquis of Willingdon, Viceroy of India from 1931-1936. Like her elder sister, Marie also clearly took an active part in her husband's career. A keen golfer, the Marquis is famously quoted as saying of his wife: "I thought I married a Brassey, but instead she turned out to be a driver."

So it was amongst this highly unconventional and socially aware family that the young Buck, only two, along with his two elder sisters, Idina and Avice, were to live following his mother's divorce from the eighth Earl in 1902. Leaving the Manor House, where she had orchestrated so much of the development of Bexhill with her former husband, Muriel returned first to Normanhurst Court, her parents' sprawling Victorian mansion near Bexhill (and the house where Buck had been born), and then to Old Lodge, Hartfield, Sussex, and various homes in London.

Muriel had already spent much of her life surrounded by political visionaries. Gladstone had been a frequent visitor to her parents' home and, in 1885, even sailed with them on the *The Sunbeam* to Norway while recuperating from an illness. But while her family (and she, initially) were supporters of the Liberals, her forthright support of women's suffrage led her to join the Labour Party, and fight actively for women's rights.

With her younger sister, Lady Helen, and her daughter Idina, she founded the East Grinstead Suffrage Union and was president of the

The eighth Earl and his family

The ninth Earl aged 8 years

Normanhurst Court, c1880

Suffrage Society for Hastings, St Leonards and East Sussex. Her commitment towards social change ran deeper than mere tokenism. A close friend, George Lansbury, the Labour MP for Poplar, later claimed that Countess De La Warr played a very important role in both the feminist and socialist movements but "it was little known because she always insisted on being kept in the background".[3]

According to Lansbury, Muriel used her position and money to help support not only the campaign for women's suffrage, but also trade union rights and self-determination for India. "When in 1911–12 the London dock workers were on strike, and indeed whenever any great or small body of workers were suffering, she would raise money and hand it on anonymously, sometimes through myself and sometimes through others, to help the workers win. Over and over again she and her friends saved the *Daily Herald* from death in the old days when it was independent. Her love for human rights and duties kept her very largely out of society. She spent her days almost secretly doing good."[4]

Muriel's belief that, both through example and her actions, she could influence public morality is clearly echoed in her son. Like other contemporaries, she also believed this moral offensive had a more spiritual side, and became closely involved with the workings of the Theosophical Society, a quasi-religious organisation founded on the concepts of physical and spiritual perfection through reincarnation leading to the periodic manifestation of divine beings on Earth, Jesus Christ being one. The teachings were to have a direct impact on family life at the De La Warr home.

At the time, the Theosophists believed that a new Messiah had arrived in the form of a young Indian boy named Krishnamurti, 'discovered' some years earlier by the Society's President, the writer and campaigner Annie Besant. In 1911, Besant brought the sixteen year-old Messiah to London with his brother, Nitya, trailing them with her on presentations and lectures, to undertake studies in preparation for a British (and preferably Oxbridge) university education.[5]

The new Messiah and his brother spent much of their stay in England with Muriel and her family at the house to which they had recently moved, Old Lodge, in the Ashdown Forest. Krishnamurti was 17, and the young Buck, 13. As a result of Lady De La Warr's beneficence, they were to spend much time together over the coming years.

Krishna's father, from whom Besant had taken the boys, started a lengthy and high-profile legal battle for their return. To keep them out of the media spotlight, the boys were dispatched to Sussex while the case was fought out, ultimately, by the highest courts in both India and England. The fight was at last won by the campaigning Mrs Besant but the unsavoury publicity it aroused meant the authorities refused the boys entry to Oxford. True to character, however, Lady De La Warr stuck by them, taking a house in Wimbledon in 1915 for herself and the two boys while her own son, at only 16, went off to war.

The episode, and its indication of Lady De La Warr's commitment to spiritual and socialist principles, is certain to have had a profound impact on the family and, in particular, the young Earl. It explains his vegetarianism – a principle he maintained until much later in life when, according to his daughter Kitty, he raided the fridge one day at the family home, devoured a leg of chicken and never looked back.

It explains his pacifist views. Keen to serve his country in World War I, Buck left Eton at just 16, enlisting in the Royal Naval Reserve with a posting on board a minesweeper. While still very much in the war – and a highly dangerous task – it was, nevertheless, a role dedicated to saving lives rather than taking them away.

It also sheds light on the young Earl's clearly-held left-wing view of social enterprise, civic duty and humanitarian values. However, not only were these principles to guide the ninth Earl throughout his life: they formed the foundation for much of the thinking behind both the modernist and socialist movements on the rise throughout the 1920s and 30s, and in which formation the ninth Earl himself played no small part.

Earl and Countess De La Warr at
Buckhurst Farm, Withyham, c1960

The rise to influence

Although he inherited his title at 15, the young Earl De La Warr did not officially start to take over his new responsibilities until the end of World War I when, at 18, he first presented himself at Parliament. Even then, however, his distinctive character was to the fore. Sitting on the steps of the Throne, the place reserved for peers who have succeeded as minors and so who cannot yet take their official place in the Upper Chamber, the young Socialist was to eschew the ermine and velvet of his peers wearing, instead, his able-bodied seaman's uniform. Unbeknownst to Buck, it was a historic first, another in both his family's long past and his own future.

More surprises were in store. As soon as he was able to take his seat he became an active member of the Labour Party to which his mother had earlier become a devotee. As such, he became the first hereditary peer to represent the new party in the Lords – a foundation stone for far greater influence in future years.

He went to Oxford, studying agriculture at Magdalen College, developing a skill and understanding of the subject which was to serve him well throughout his life and career as both politician and farmer. And, despite his studies and parliamentary duties, he still found time to court and marry – at only 20 – proposing to his wife-to-be, Diana Leigh, in Carcassone while touring French cathedral cities in an ancient Ford car with fellow pilgrims David Crawford, Mark van Oss and Lord Gladwyn.

Diana was the daughter of a captain in the Life Guards, and had clearly been raised in the traditions of duty and public service. She and Buck were to remain married for 46 years – despite Buck's renowned 'eye for the women' – and there is little doubt the Earl's achievements were due, in no small part, to having a devoted and supportive wife at home. Harold Nicolson, his cousin through Nicolson's marriage to Vita Sackville-West, would have been the first to agree. Writing while Minister for Information, Nicolson mused to his wife: "What bothers me is whether I have given way too much to your eccentricities. Some outside person might imagine I should have made more of my life if I had had someone like Diana De La Warr to share my career..."[6]

In the early 1920s, though, the new pair had the world at their feet. So impressed had the then Prime Minister, Ramsay MacDonald, been of his new Labour peer he brought him into the Government just four years later, in 1924. Choosing him to move the Address to the House of Lords, MacDonald made De La Warr a Lord-in-Waiting, and a Government Whip, too.

He remained a Whip while the Socialists were out of power from 1924–1929 but, on MacDonald's return to No.10, De La Warr was again appointed a Lord-in-Waiting, and also became Under-Secretary of State for War, holding both positions concurrently. He was not to be long in the post: a ministerial reshuffle saw the Earl move to become Parliamentary Secretary in the Ministry of Agriculture, a position where he could draw on both his education in agriculture and his background as a Sussex farmer. As such, he was able to introduce a series of valuable measures in the House of Lords and start off an involvement in the development of modern British agriculture which was to continue throughout his life.

The precise nature – and extent – of the Earl's influence in the politics of the day is only lightly chronicled. Certainly, he never rose to the prominence enjoyed by many of his contemporaries; the MacDonalds, Churchill, Boothby or even Harold Nicolson. However, at the important moments in the history of the period, his name crops up regularly.

In the controversies which split the Labour Party in 1931, De La Warr chose to stick with Ramsay MacDonald. But neither he – nor MacDonald – were to be out in the wilderness for long. Returning swiftly to power, MacDonald once again appointed De La Warr to his old job in the Agriculture Ministry when he formed his second National Government in November 1931, a position the Earl was to retain until being transferred to the Board of Education as Parliamentary Secretary four years later. In the same year, at just 31, De La Warr was to move towards the very heart of political influence, becoming chairman of the newly-formed National Labour Party. It was a task which, over the next twelve years, saw him bring many new politicians into the fold, including his cousin Harold Nicolson for whom he was to find the safe seat of West Leicester to contest and win.

But how had this young man, half the age of most of his colleagues, managed to manoeuvre his way through political turbulence and upset with such finesse? How had this wealthy aristocrat negotiated his way to high political office in Government at a time when Socialism, with its modern outlook and philosophies was capturing the people's imagination?

The answers are manifold. Delve deeper into the mood and character of the times and a clearer picture emerges of the reasons the young Earl was able to achieve so much. He was, quite simply, a man whose time had come.

Britain in the 1930s
The rise of Modernism

De La Warr moved amongst the intelligentsia of Britain. His good friend Ivor Churchill, with whom he had studied at both Eton and Oxford, was the son of the Duke of Marlborough and his American wife Consuela Vanderbilt, his inherited fortune enabling him to become one of the country's leading art collectors, an expertise he often lent to De La Warr in his own acquisitions. The Earl's social circle read like a who's who of English Society at the time: shipping heiress Emerald Cunard, Evelyn Waugh, Oswald Mosley and his wife Diana (Mitford) to name but a few. Parties at Sybil Colefax's saw Buck dining with the young King Edward VIII and Mrs Simpson, Kenneth Clarke, Oscar Rubinstein, Winston and Clementine Churchill, Diana Cooper and the ever-entertaining Noel Coward.

To the friendly ears of both Royalty, Government, and the Arts, De La Warr was able to bring an unconventional, almost exotic upbringing, an awareness of the rights of ordinary human beings, and yet ancestry, wealth and power dating back 700 years. In short, characteristics which captured the essence of the times.

Much was changing around him. The General Strike of 1926 was a premonition of the troubles that were unleashed following the Wall Street Crash in the autumn of 1929. Britain's adherence to the Gold Standard since 1925 had become a divisive issue, favouring financiers but leaving manufacturers over-priced in the international markets for their goods, and when Prime Minister Ramsay MacDonald abandoned the link in November 1931, some saw it as a betrayal of the promises he had made when forming the National Government – with De La Warr as chairman of the party – just three months before. More generally, it seems to have acted as a catalyst for the intellectual classes, who became more engaged with the politics of Britain, identifying a need for a general modernisation of society and its infrastructure.

It was a time when England could easily have swayed towards either Communism or Fascism, both of which were building in Continental Europe. Industrial Britain, however, sought a more pragmatic solution to its problems with forward-looking projects such as the De La Warr Pavilion.

At the time, few intellectuals had taken a direct interest in architecture, yet many were now becoming aware of the deteriorating condition of the environment, as roadside advertising and the sprawling 'ribbon-development' around towns sprung up, particularly in southern England. The BBC commissioned a series of influential talks from advocates of better design, with proponents such as Frank Pick, whose commissions for the London Underground had made it famous as a public organisation whose coherent visual policy matched and furthered its operational efficiency. As a result, modern design in Britain during the 1930s emerged as a strange amalgam of conservatism and progress, incorporating art with industry and inspired by almost mediaeval ideas of an organic society.

It was Continental Europe that provided the strongest visual inspiration for the new concepts. Pick, with his architect, Charles Holden, studied modern buildings in Holland, Germany and Sweden in the summer of 1930, culminating in a visit, along with many other British architects and designers, to the influential Stockholm Exhibition. There, they saw the playful, slender pavilions and restaurants designed by Erik Gunnar Asplund who, having designed elegant neo-classical buildings throughout the 1920s, went spectacularly modern in 1930.

It inspired the English. Spurred by the same optimism in building, new designs started to emerge as the English came to see modern design as something they too could excel in. The trend had been happening all over Europe, but when Hitler came to power in 1933 the Nazis condemned modern architecture as alien and 'bolshevik'. Erich Mendelsohn whose Jewish identity made him doubly at risk, was one of many who fled the country. Along with other manifestations of liberal culture, Modernism and the architecture it promoted became synonymous with left-wing politics.

Like any influential movement, what started as a political trend soon also became fashionable, confirming its success, as critic Gavin Stamp explains: "Particularly after the appointment of Hitler as Chancellor in 1933, the Modern Movement associated itself with democracy as well as progress; not to subscribe to its position and style became, by definition, reactionary if not 'fascist'…to be anything but a committed modernist became as unfashionable and as unacceptable to the young as to support non-intervention in Spain."[7]

Young, titled, and at the heart of both society and politics, few individuals in the 30s were in a better position to push forward the ideals of the new movement than the ninth Earl De La Warr. In 1933, he set to work.

The De La Warr Pavilion

The demand for a new, large entertainments venue for the growing town of Bexhill was apparent years earlier than the eventual scheme which saw the construction of the world-class modernist Pavilion which now bears its instigator's name.

From 1907 various proposals were made for a 'Winter Garden' or some form of large enclosed entertainment hall. Sites proposed had included Egerton Park, the area owned by John Webb, The Kursaal, built by the eighth Earl, while bands also sometimes played at the Colonnade on Bexhill's seafront, another site mooted.

A report commissioned by the local Bexhill Corporation from Adams, Thompson & Fry in 1930 advocated a radical redevelopment of the whole borough, including proposals for a 'music pavilion and enlarged band enclosure' on the Colonnade site. Plans were drawn up and a £50,000 scheme proposed for an entertainments hall, museum, library and reading room, but the development ran into the ground over long-standing disputes – still being fought to this day – between those who saw the town's future as solely residential and those who wished to develop it as a resort. Only when the town's newly-elected mayor picked up the challenge was the contest to move any nearer to its conclusion.

Although already a Government Minister, chairman of his party, and owner of the family farming estates, the energetic Earl De La Warr was keen to continue the tradition of both his father and grandfather by becoming, in addition, Mayor of Bexhill. Ever pragmatic, perhaps in the Edwardian seaside town the new young modernist could finally put his ideas into practice with bricks and mortar.

In 1933 the new Mayor set to work, delicately balancing the tricky politics of the town with a process of public consultation for the new pavilion, finally courting overwhelming public support for the proposals. At its centre, the debate wrangled over whether the project should be financed privately or met by public funds. The socialist Earl's determination was clear, and won through: "My own view is that if it is going to pay private enterprise, it is going to pay the town."[8]

After much discussion it was finally agreed, in April 1933, that the Corporation should develop the seafront site themselves by erecting an entertainments hall at a cost of no more than £50,000 and, in a clever move to divert further public criticism, that they should ask the Royal Institute of British Architects to run an open competition for the project, with an appointed assessor.

While the Corporation was clearly the official body through which the decisions were taken, De La Warr's hand is evident throughout in both the nature of the contest and its eventual, modernist solution. Firstly, the decision to run a competition was, in itself, a radical one. Few contests had been held for public buildings, and never before on such a scale.

The assessor chosen by the RIBA to oversee the competition was also, himself, a modernist architect. Thomas Tait was an early champion of the movement in Britain, having designed, amongst other buildings, a number of modern houses for Critall, the metal-window manufacturer, at Silver End in Essex in 1926-7 and the Royal Masonic Hospital in Ravenscourt Park (1930-33), itself the result of a competition. A partner in the respected firm of Burnet, Tait and Lorne, Tait was at once acknowledged by the older generation of architects and regarded as open-minded by the younger.[9]

And the architectural brief, too, was clear in its intention that the eventual solution should be in the modern style: "simple in design...obtained by the use of large window spaces, terraces and canopies...light in appearance." It continued: " Heavy stonework is not desirable...modern steel-framed or ferro-concrete construction may be adopted..."[10] But, as the ninth Earl himself clearly knew, the design of a modernist building is one thing. Getting it built is an altogether different challenge.

Due to the relative under-employment of architects at the time, the competition attracted a phenomenal 230 entries. The winner, as is well-known, was the new British partnership of Germany's Erich Mendelsohn and society high-flyer, Russian-born Serge Chermayeff.

Certainly, the young Earl would have met Chermayeff socially before. It was Chermayeff who brought into the practice most of the work he and Mendelsohn were to carry out during their partnership's all-too-brief existence, through his extensive social and professional contacts. But any suggestion the contest was anything if not proper was quickly scotched by De La Warr. Several local residents objected to the appointment of foreign architects to design and build a British public building, some even writing to the Town Clerk saying so. Their letters brought a swift reply from the Mayor, retorting: "You are no doubt aware that in a competition of this character no one, not even the Council or the Assessor himself, knows the names of the competitors until the award has actually been made."

Other wrangles were to ensue. Although a budget ceiling had been set at £50,000, Mendelsohn and Chermayeff had costed their initial design at £58,000. In addition, the Council were to decide subsequently that it wanted a fully-equipped stage and that the Colonnade should be reconstructed to accommodate a proposed swimming pool. This, together with Chermayeff's proposals for windows to be made of rust-resistant bronze, a Frank Dobson statue and other expenses had pushed the total bill up to £80,000.

Writing for *Modern British Architecture* in 1987, Cyril Sweett, the project's quantity surveyor, recalled the mood: "The design of the building was not to the liking of the local residents, most of whom were retired service people. Lord De La Warr, who was Mayor of Bexhill at the time, was, however, a powerful figure with a distinct preference for the design and, I think, a personal friendship with Chermayeff, and he insisted the scheme should proceed. The opposition, however, insisted that there should be a public inquiry and an inspector was appointed to conduct it in Bexhill."[10]

Nevertheless, despite a protracted inquiry and a scaling-down of the plans to reduce the overall cost, De La Warr got his way. With a contract stating that construction must be completed within fifty weeks and that as many local builders as possible should be used in the process, work started on the new Pavilion in January 1935. An architectural revolution was under way.

From the start, it became clear the De La Warr Pavilion was no ordinary building. It was the first major welded steel frame building of its kind to be constructed in Britain; the strange steel skeleton rising rapidly on Bexhill's seafront owed much to Mendelsohn's pioneering engineer Felix Samuely who had developed the technique

De La Warr Pavilion, east elevation, c1936

De La Warr Pavilion under construction, 1935

in Germany. While it may have paved the way for techniques now commonplace around the world, in sleepy Bexhill in the 1930s it cast an odd shadow indeed.

Not for the building's originators the mud and slime of the building site, either. Headquarters for the operation, instead, were the elegant surroundings of the Cooden Beach Hotel, owned and run by the ninth Earl's wife Diana. Here, the team of builders, architects and engineers developing the Pavilion gathered for meetings to discuss progress with the construction just a couple of miles along the coast.

Few building sites are worthy of a Royal visit, either, but Earl De La Warr's new Pavilion was one. Visiting his Lord-in-Waiting for lunch at the Cooden Beach, King George V and Queen Mary were so taken with the model of the planned Pavilion the Earl had showed them, a visit to the building site was hurriedly arranged.

Though Buck's ability to marry policy and patronage was working wonders, it was clearly no accident. Laying a plaque at the Pavilion in May to commemorate the King's Silver Jubilee, he said: "In doing so I mark a great day in the history of Bexhill, for which we have rightly chosen a great day in the history of our nation. How better could we dedicate ourselves today than by gathering round this new venture of ours, a venture which is going to lead to the growth, the prosperity and the greater culture of this, our town."

Significantly, he was to add: "A venture also which is part of a great national movement virtually to found a new industry – the industry of giving that relaxation, that pleasure, that culture, which hitherto the gloom and dreariness of British resorts has driven our fellow countrymen to seek in foreign lands." Like so many buildings which

Earl De La Warr (right) with King George V and Countess
De La Warr (left) with Queen Mary visiting the De La Warr
Pavilion during construction, 1935

Earl De La Warr and his family during the laying of the foundation stone for the
De La Warr Pavilion, 1935

were to follow it, Earl De La Warr's new Pavilion had a social, as well as architectural purpose.

Tight deadline or no, construction was completed absolutely on schedule and, on 12 December 1935, the De La Warr Pavilion was opened by the Duke and Duchess of York, themselves to be crowned soon after. Touchingly, the future Queen was presented with a bouquet by the Earl's young daughter, Lady Kitty Sackville. Yet in characteristic De La Warr family fashion, she would only agree to present the bouquet if she could be accompanied, not by some lady-in-waiting or dowager-like nanny, but by her friend Captain Jim Stevens of the Bexhill Fire Brigade, which had recently named their fire engine after her. While it could never be anything other than aristocratic, rarely does the ninth Earl De La Warr or his family ever appear to lose touch with the proletariat.

Reaction to the building was swift and, in the main, laudatory. Describing it as 'the most satisfactory example of modern architecture I have seen in this country', the *New Statesman* commented: "You could not find a stronger argument in favour of town planning than Bexhill, which is not so much a town as a chaotic litter of hideous houses sprawling higgledy-piggledy along a lovely coast. Lord De La Warr, whose ancestors were responsible for this muddle has now made an act of reparation."

"By far the most civilised thing that has been done on the South Coast since the days of the Regency," said the *Times*. Professor Reilly wrote in the *Manchester Guardian*: "When one looks at the plain cream surfaces, divided by long vertical lines, to define the inevitable graduations in colour, one wonders whether we are yet ready, and particularly whether Bexhill is yet ready, for such elegance."

From the day it opened, the De La Warr Pavilion caused controversy, much of which still rages today. "I am no admirer of this Epstein stuff," barked Bexhill resident Sir Duncombe Mann, one of a number of local residents opposed to the building, sounding off in the *Daily Mirror*.

Indeed, so sensitive to the delicate nature of popular opinion within the Borough was Earl De La Warr that he took the unprecedented step of *turning down* the freedom of the Borough when it was offered to him in 1936 for his three years of invaluable service to the town. "It would naturally be pleasing to receive such an honour, feeling that it was with the approval of the Burgesses of Bexhill, but whilst so much controversy about the Pavilion still exists, there would evidently be a certain number who would once again condemn the action of the council," he stated.

Without doubt, the 'controversy' referred to, centred largely on the shock of the new – a stark, cream building, the like of which had rarely been seen before in the country and, certainly, never on such a scale. But to focus only on the appearance of the building is to overlook one of its original precepts – that of the power of architecture in social terms, as well as visual.

The influential philosopher-scientist J D Bernal, who was in frequent dialogue with Serge Chermayeff at the time, wrote: "The function of all buildings is pre-eminently social, rather than biological utility". Perhaps lost over time, but it was this social commitment which so set the De La Warr Pavilion apart as a true exercise in Modernism.

That this was due, in no small part, to the Earl's own vision is also now recognised. Stephen Bayley, writing in *Britain in the Thirties* : "Earl De La Warr, Mayor of Bexhill, and Chairman of the National Labour Party, wanted to build a socialist palace by the sea… The Pavilion, combining resort places with elements of popularising, patronising culture, provided the architects with the opportunity to build in England's homely south coast what continental Europe and Soviet Russia had not then yet realised: briefly, at Bexhill, under aristocratic patronage, building technology and moralising architecture came together in the service of the people."[11]

Controversial or not, Buck had managed to build a lasting testament to the new order of his time. Bold, forward-looking and borne of a philosophy that architecture – and the design of architecture – should serve a function beyond the visual to involve both moral and social issues, the De La Warr Pavilion has rightly been coined 'the people's palace'.

But it was not the only bold move Earl De La Warr was to initiate for the people he clearly cared so deeply for. Though the Pavilion was complete, Buck had only just begun. He was, after all, only 36.

A hand in history

A highly visible member of the National Labour party for some ten years, De La Warr's march through the ranks of Government was nearly complete. In 1935, he had been transferred from his post as Parliamentary Secretary at the Agriculture Ministry to the same post at the Board of Education, but promotion was soon to follow.

After eight months in office at Education, he was promoted to be Under-Secretary of State for the Colonies and, in May 1937, entered Neville Chamberlain's Cabinet as Lord Privy Seal, being sworn in as a Privy Councillor.

His posts had not, until then, been of the highest order, but he had kept a central position in the politics of the era via his chairmanship of the National Labour Party. In June of 1935, the Conservative Stanley Baldwin had succeeded Ramsay MacDonald as Prime Minister in the then National Government. The Earl was chairman of the co-ordination committee established to allocate seats between the three component parties of the Government; Conservative, National Labour and Liberal.

Though the Government enjoyed the title of 'National', few could escape the fact that any other influence in it other than Conservative was very small indeed. The National Labour Party held cabinet posts through De La Warr, J H Thomas and both Ramsay and Malcolm MacDonald, his son, the October election had seen Baldwin win with a massive 425 seats, 385 of which were Conservative, 32 National Liberal and only 8 National Labour.

In his famous diaries, Harold Nicolson recalls how important De La

Warr was to Baldwin's continuing success. Meeting him on the day of King George V's funeral, in January 1936: "We discussed the future of the National Labour party and agreed there is none. Two MacDonalds (Ramsay and Malcolm) have fought bye-elections with the aid of Tory Central Office and we cannot claim independence. But Baldwin wants to maintain a semblance of a National Government and wants us to help."[12]

That the National Government remained in office, first under Baldwin and then under Chamberlain, until the onset of War owes much to the sensitive politicking of Earl De La Warr. Though he may have disagreed privately with Chamberlain – whom he believed to be weak and ineffectual – Buck was nothing if not discreet and loyal.

In public, therefore, as both Lord Privy Seal and chairman of the National Labour Party his support was practical – and influential. As Chamberlain's Government stumbled from crisis to crisis during 1938, De La Warr presided over a meeting of the whole National Labour Executive, drawing up a paper of support for the Government, against which voted only Churchill and Harold Nicolson. While the debate raged over Hitler's Germany, De La Warr knew only too well the importance of unity in the face of adversity.

In private, however, Buck was more vocal. Pragmatic as ever, his views were driven more by the desire for practical action and results than any partisan allegiance. In cabinet meetings De La Warr was quoted as saying he would face war to free the world from the constant threat of ultimata, a view which found little support among the peacemongering Chamberlain Government. This may explain his demotion to the less prestigious office of President of the Board of Education, though he remained in the cabinet.

By August the following year, De La Warr was already discussing 'when' war might come, rather than 'if', according to Nicolson. He was also trying to figure "a more active job than that of a Cabinet Minister"[12] once it had been declared, even if it meant leaving the Government. He was not to have to wait long.

In the fateful events which led Britain for the second time in two decades to war with Germany, De La Warr's role, if not leading, must certainly have been influential. According to Nicholson's diaries, the Earl was deeply pessimistic about the prospects for peace so laboured by his colleagues. Instead, he saw Chamberlain's Munich agreement with Hitler as mere delaying tactics, and when Chamberlain proposed a diplomatic conference as war became ever more imminent in 1939, it was more of the same.

However, he was one of just six ministers to force their beleaguered Prime Minister's hand. Rather than supporting Chamberlain's proposals set out in the House of Commons on 2nd September 1939, it was the acting Labour leader, Arthur Greenwood's exhortation to action which struck the right note in De La Warr's camp.

'Greenwood went to Chamberlain and told him that, unless war were declared next morning, 'it would be impossible to hold the House', wrote historian A J P Taylor. Later that evening, De La Warr was to meet in Chancellor Sir John Simon's room with War Secretary Leslie Hore-Belisha, a National Liberal MP, Labour's Sir John Anderson, W.Eliot, and Lord Minney to discuss the crisis. 'Simon carried their message to Chamberlain: war must be declared at once'.[13]

The cabinet met at 11pm that night. According to Taylor, some members of it declared they would not leave the room until an immediate ultimatum was sent to Germany – the very message to have come out of De La Warr's meeting in Sir John Simon's room. 'Chamberlain gloomily agreed... The British ultimatum was delivered to the German government at 9am on 3rd September 1939. The Germans made no reply, and the ultimatum expired at 11am.' Britain was at war.

Once again, a De La Warr baron was to be present at one of the turning points of history. Like many of his forefathers and, indeed, not for the first time himself, Buck had followed his instincts and acted decisively, rather than follow slavishly the machinery of party politics. And not long after his crucial involvement in those fateful events, he was to get the 'more active job' he sought, becoming the first Commissioner of Works as Britain prepared for battle.

De La Warr's war

As for so many of his countrymen, the second World War brought the ninth Earl both triumph and tragedy. His hand had helped decide the fate of Britain for the next six years, and he continued to serve his country in whatever way he could, albeit not at the centre of power.

Yet this was also a difficult time for the energetic peer. His sister, Lady Idina Sackville, was involved in a much-publicised scandal after her former husband, the Earl of Errol, was found slain at the wheel of his car in Africa. His long-held allegiance to the National Labour Party he had helped to establish wavered and failed. His eldest son, William, Lord Buckhurst, was heavily involved in the fighting, distinguishing himself in the parachute landings at Arnhem and El Alamein. And his beloved younger son, Harry, went missing in action, his body never to be recovered.

At the outbreak of war, however, De La Warr remained in the cabinet, as President of the Board of Education. And, though he was not to know it at the time, he was to play a significant part in yet another important milestone in British history of the twentieth century – the eventual creation of both the 1951 Festival of Britain and of the Arts Council, the key government agency still responsible for the direction of the arts throughout the country to this day. The story is typical of the creative energy he brought to so many of his posts.

With theatres and concert halls closed, the country in enforced black-out, large numbers of the population were spending each evening huddled together in air-raid shelters and cellars with little to do except dwell on fear. De La Warr, keen to find a way to still bring art and entertainment to the people despite war-time conditions, met the Chairman of the Pilgrim Trust, Lord Macmillan, then also Minister for Information, to ask whether the Trust could provide a grant for an idea to help alleviate the public's frustration. They met in Macmillan's room on December 14th 1939.[14]

"Lord De La Warr was enthusiastic. He had Venetian visions of a post-war Lord Mayor's show on the Thames in which the Board of Education led the arts in triumph from Whitehall to Greenwich in magnificent barges and gorgeous gondolas: orchestras, madrigal singers, Shakespeare from the Old Vic, ballet from Sadler's Wells, shining canvasses from the Royal Academy, folk dancers from village greens – in fact, Merrie England. Lord Macmillan's grave judicial calm collapsed suddenly and completely. At the moment he was responsible for national morale, and in the President's dream he saw employment for actors singers and painters, and refreshment for the multitude of war workers for the duration. Supply and demand kissed. Would £25,000 be of any use?"[15]

The Chairman of the Pilgrim Trust was to honour his promise, supporting De La Warr's 'idea' which, though he himself had moved on, was to lead to the establishment of the Council for the Encouragement of Music and the Arts (CEMA).

CEMA's valuable role in providing the hoped-for artistic refreshment for a war-shattered Britain was taken on in peace time by the newly-formed Arts Council which itself developed De La Warr's germ of an idea for a Thameside festival into the 1951 Festival of Britain. Though he was not to know it at the time, his vision of a river festival was to develop into a hugely influential celebration of science and the arts, engineering the rise of London's South Bank in the arts world, and spawning the industry of arts festivals promoted so successfully today.

Though he moved from Education in April the following year, Buck's 'more active' job as Commissioner of Works was not to last long. The onset of war was, of course, the end of Chamberlain. De La Warr failed to find a place in Churchill's coalition government of May 1940, in all probability for the simple fact that the Labour Party had never fully forgiven him for joining Ramsay MacDonald's National Government in 1931: the split which resulted had driven Labour (as distinct from National Labour) into Opposition for ten years.

However, the early ideals of National Labour were wearing thin on the party's chairman, too. In 1943, twelve years after he had first presided over the party he helped establish, the ninth Earl resigned his post and left the party.

For such a committed socialist, the move must surely have been taken with a heavy heart, yet it is not entirely out of character. As close friend and colleague Sir Colin Coote explains, although the political label of 'National Labour' might have been invented for De La Warr: "He always recoiled from dogma in any and every walk of life".[16] Clearly, with a war on, De La Warr had had enough of the bickering between parties which so often besets coalition governments.

Whether driven by ideological concerns, therefore, or by a more a more realistic desire to return to practical administration, The Earl's decision did not go unnoticed. Soon after, he was appointed Director of Home Flax Production at the Ministry of Supply, signalling a return to his former familiar stamping ground of agriculture.

His ability to bridge political divides was always to serve him well. Many treat those who leave one political party to join another – as Buck was to do by joining the Conservatives in 1945 – as little more than traitors. However, it says a great deal for the continued goodwill he mustered amongst his former Labour colleagues that, despite his switch of party allegiance, he remained as head of flax production in the Supply Ministry for four years, even after Clement Attlee's Labour Government was elected after the war in 1945.

His particular brand of diplomacy was also used directly by Churchill during the war itself, after he was dispatched to negotiate an agreement for the continuance of the British Military Mission in Ethiopia. Although eventually successful, the delegation proved to challenge every ounce of De La Warr's understanding of the human (and Ethiopian) condition.

Reporting to Foreign Secretary Anthony Eden, he was quick to realise that the Ethiopians... "Know their real dependence on us...they are surrounded by us... they need our Military Mission...and they need and will have to have our financial help."[17]

But he was also highly sensitive to the reasons his delegation's task was to prove so difficult: "There is no question we have let them down badly on advisers in the past... Wherever she has had a good type of Englishman... she appreciates them and accepts their advice. On the other hand, a second-rate Englishman...is seen through at once."

Large tracts of land were at stake. The continued support of a key nation in Africa hung in the balance. And Britain's position, not as the old Imperialist coloniser but as the new architect of a post-war order, was vital to uphold. However, as De La Warr was to discover in his discussions with the Emperor Haile Selassie, racial attitudes were also at play. A lesser man may have ignored the subtleties so crucial to secure the agreements required.

"The Emperor himself spoke to me more than once about this matter. In every British house with 'boys' who speak English and at every bar in Addis (Abbaba, the capital), there is nothing but abuse of the 'Habash' (the local, coloured population). In Nairobi and Eritrea it is very much the same. Social intercourse is almost completely absent. The colour bar is almost complete."

Sternly, he recommended: "This should not be allowed to continue. A definite lead must be given to these British communities that so long as we desire to work in this country such action is prejudicial to our interests."

Perhaps sitting in a drawer somewhere in the De La Warr family's estate in Sussex lies the gold cigarette case presented to the Earl by the Emperor as a parting gift once negotiation had been secured. Certainly, it was but a token in exchange for the Rolls-Royce De La Warr presented the Emperor with on behalf of the Government on his departure. But the blend of good humour and political skill which so characterised Buck's achievements has never been more accurately described than by his colleagues who worked along side him during the 1944 mission.

Bundled together with the archive of his work is a selection of humourous verse written by one 'W.A.M.D', an otherwise anonymous member of the delegation.

Your patience, tact and sunny charm,
Which critics could not but disarm,
Your kindness and consideration,
Won over all your Delegation

It was no mere accident that De La Warr had been chosen to visit Africa to negotiate with Selassie. In addition to his evident diplomacy, De La Warr had been a frequent visitor to the continent for many years. In 1937, while Under-Secretary of State for the Colonies, he had also spent ten weeks as chairman of a Government Commission sent out to report on African education, touring both with his wife, Diana, and Harold Nicolson, a member of the Commission. Later in life he was to buy land there himself and, like his ancestors before him, grow tobacco.

He also had close links to Africa through his sister, Lady Idina, who had moved to Kenya with her new husband, the future Earl of Errol, in 1924. Unfortunately, the episode ended in tragedy.

Idina was seven years older than Buck. Much like her brother, by all accounts, she was irresistible to the opposite sex, a trait which she used to outrageous effect, hosting scandalously louche parties in the so-called 'Happy Valley' of similarly-minded English expatriates in Kenya. The couple had a daughter, Dinan, but were soon to divorce, Dinan being dispatched back to Britain to live with her aunt, Buck's other sister, Lady Avice Spicer, in Wiltshire.

But by 1941, events had taken a sinister turn. Early one January morning, Dinan's father was found slain at the wheel of his Buick, a bullet lodged in the back of his head. The suspect, never proven, was a wealthy landowner – Sir Jock Delves Broughton – with whose wife Erroll had been having an affair. The trial hit the headlines back in Britain. England was scandalised. Dinan learn of her father's death through the papers. Although she was now Countess of Errol, her family never discussed the events surrounding her father's death with her. [18]

This apparent inability to discuss emotions, questions or even, in this case, facts surrounding tragedy affecting a family is an altogether English trait – the 'stiff upper lip' – and one all-too-familiar to the English upper classes of the time. It does not, however, signify those emotions are not actually felt, as they clearly were with the disappearance of the Earl's second son, Harry, reported missing in action in 1943.

"The loss of (Buck's) younger son in the Second World War was a blow from which, I think, rightly or wrongly, he never fully recovered. At least, it seemed to cast a veil over a former exuberant character." Close friend he may have been, yet even Sir Colin Coote (who penned these words in his obituary to Earl De La Warr in 1976) could only speculate over the heavy impact of the tragedy on this most English of aristocrats.

But while he may have found it difficult to express his emotions, it doesn't mean the ninth Earl wasn't at least interested in trying. Much to the annoyance and dislike of his children, De La Warr was highly interested in the new science of psychiatry, and subjected both himself and his family to a journey of self-discovery for many years.

Buck had been introduced to the science by his close friend Ivor Churchill and was a fervent believer in its capabilities. His daughter, Kitty, was psychoanalysed daily for ten years by the famous post-

Freudian analyst Melanie Klein from the incredibly young age of three. Recalling her father, she relates: "He used to say 'If I can't have my children psychoanalysed I won't have children'. I think it was because he felt that children pop out fairly clear of context and difficulty and he was damned well going to keep them that way."

It wasn't the most popular of family activities, however. "My brothers went until they were eight or nine but they got off because they went to prep. school and I was landed with it until the second World War saved me. He even made my poor mother go, too, though she gave it up, I believe. I went. You did what you were told." And of her analyst? "It certainly taught me how to hate. I never hated anyone so much as her," she added.

Ninth Earl De La Warr with Haile Selasse, 1944
Reproduced by kind permission of the East Sussex County Archivist

Back in the fold

Like so many other aspects of life, war had sapped the confidence, the idealism of the age that had preceded it. The heady, forward-thinking era of the Thirties, and the modernist, socialist concepts which had so driven De La Warr and his contemporaries before the war now lay in tatters, as Britain toiled to dig itself out of a war-ravaged bunker. In the ninth Earl, too, idealism had given way to realism.

In December 1945, he wrote to Winston Churchill, himself cruelly ousted from power by Clement Attlee in the General Election just one month after leading Britain to victory over Germany, explaining his decision to join the Conservative party. "For the past few years I have belonged to no party, but I have been compelled to my decision by the policy of the present Government, which would seem to be to impose the shackles of doctrinaire Socialism on our economic life instead of tackling the grave and imminent problems that face us." As ever, Buck wanted to see real, practical results from his efforts.

Churchill welcomed the former National Labour cabinet minister to the Conservatives, saying it "will prove to be a true People's Party in the years that lie before us." After just a few short years of self-imposed exile, the Earl, often regarded as a maverick, was back in political favour, even if it was still to be a further six years before he returned to political office. Unlike his elected colleagues, however, the hereditary peer's seat at Westminster wasn't tested at the polls every four to five years. He could afford to wait.

Still working as Director of Home Flax Production, he returned his attention to agriculture and his own farms in Sussex. In London, the family maintained a house in Chester Square. However, in Sussex, rather than live at the Buckhurst Estate mansion, the ninth Earl preferred the rather less grand (but still very comfortable) Fishersgate adjoining his model farm at Withyham. Winnie the Pooh's immortal 'Hundred Acre Wood' ran alongside the land. His wife, Diana, had her own farm, too.

Shortly after the success of the De La Warr Pavilion competition, its architect Erich Mendelsohn worked on designs for a new house at Beaulieu, in Hampshire which, according to his assistant, Birkin Haward, were for Earl De La Warr[19]. Some of the original drawings still survive but, alas, the house itself was never built, Mendelsohn leaving soon after first for Palestine and then, eventually, the United States.

Back amongst the the rolling Sussex hills, however, Buck could indulge his passion for the countryside and experiment with new farming techniques, championing, in particular, the ley farming techniques pioneered by Sir R G Stapleton. From 1944 to 1949, he chaired the Agricultural Research Council, a key body in the development of post-war Britain out of food shortages and rationing and into the modern, mechanised food producer of today. And in 1969 he was awarded the Royal Agricultural Society's Bledisloe Gold Medal, in recognition of his work as a pioneer of mechanical farming and outstanding services to agriculture.

For such a lover of the land it was an achievement to be proud of. Yet his success in farming, just as in politics, was all touched with the traditional De La Warr humility. "I don't remember a meal without a farmer at the table," Kitty relates of life with her father at home, "he was a wonderful employer". His generosity didn't just stretch to employment, either. Having built an almost entirely new village at Withyham for his farm workers, he nevertheless was reluctant to turf them out once they had retired. "At one point he had more pensioners than workers occupying the cottages," she goes on. "That was typical of him".

Life, nevertheless, was comfortable. The De La Warrs loved entertaining: Ivor Churchill was a frequent visitor, as was Malcolm Sargent and Lord Duff and Lady Diana Cooper. And the house at Fishersgate was well supported for weekend visits, with a butler, footman, odd jobs man, cook, kitchen maid, two housemaids to attend to the rooms, gardeners for the grounds and two carpenters. According to one of their housemaids, Mabel Derry, who still lives in a tied cottage on the family estate at Withyham, the staff were called by first-names, an informality highly unusual for the times.

But the ninth Earl's political career was still far from over. By 1951, a rapidly-changing Britain had returned Churchill to power, and De La Warr was appointed Postmaster General, a post he was to retain until Churchill resigned in 1955. Though it may not have appeared, on the face of it, the most exciting of jobs, Buck, as he had found himself so often throughout his career, was in the right place at the right time.

In the 1930s, De La Warr's modernist vision had helped shape the political mood of the times, and resulted, most visibly today, in the creation of the wonderful Pavilion in Bexhill. Throughout the 1930s and 1940s his work had led him into agriculture at a time when advances in science and technology meant farming – and food supply – was progressing in leaps and bounds. But at the start of the 1950s there was a new technology – communications, telephone and television – set to rapidly take over the world. More by coincidence than design, the new Postmaster General was once again at the centre of developments.

His term of office covered one of the most dramatic periods of progress of the twentieth century in Britain's modern media and communications industry. He oversaw the introduction of a string of ground-breaking developments, including the starting of the international telex service, the development of letter-sorting machines, the planning of the national telephone numbering scheme, and the laying of the transatlantic cable from Scotland to Newfoundland (a task which brought him into contact, coincidentally, with this author's own grandfather, Frank Fairley, who acted as engineer for the project).

His time is best remembered, though, by the introduction of commercial television, a concept to meet with virulent opposition in the House of Lords which, had it not been for the calm, polite yet persistent negotiation of Earl De La Warr, could have buried for many years this vital development for Britain's future television industry.

The debate over the principles on which the Government believed commercial television might operate is regarded by many as one of the most memorable occasions in the recent history of the House of Lords. De La Warr locked horns with his opponent, Lord Hailsham, whose withering denunciation of the Government's proposals might have defeated a less able, less determined opponent. With his own brand of tact and good humour, however, De La Warr piloted the Bill through the Lords and its subsequent committee stages, appealing to critics who maintained that commercial television might corrupt and debase the nation by stating, typically, that the decency of the British people would form the best, and ultimate safeguard against falling standards. Despite this belief, he built into the Bill important prohibitions limiting the amount of advertising permissible in broadcasts, shaping independent television in the UK into what it is today.

The argument won, the amendments complete, the Bill finally received Royal Assent in 1954: a whole new industry was born. It was his parting shot in politics. The following year, when Sir Anthony Eden formed his new Government, there was no place for De La Warr. Though he was to remain a keen participant in debates at the House of Lords until his death, his life in active politics was at a close.

There was other work to do. Shortly after his removal from office he visited Delaware, the American State named after his ancestors, and received a rapturous reception when he spoke to both houses of the State Legislature in Dover, the capital of Delaware, in a session convened specially for the occasion.

Though his role as Under-Secretary of State for the Colonies had only lasted two years before the war, he retained a keen interest in the affairs of the Commonwealth, and Africa in particular. In 1956, he became chairman of the East and Central Africa Board and in 1960, as chairman of the Royal Commonwealth Society, toured the Far East and Australasia with Diana, his wife. He also entered the City, becoming chairman of the Uganda Company, and a director of Standard Bank. His work in public office was recognised at this time, too, and he was appointed GBE in the Queen's Birthday Honours list of 1956.

Throughout the 1950s he also had a key role on the National Trust as Chairman of the Estates Committee. According to his friend and colleague on the Trust, Sir John Smith, he was always "the one most interested in the public, and making it easy for the public to visit National Trust properties."

It is this humane aspect of Buck De La Warr which weaves its way through every fibre of the man's achievements, and rarely can it be seen in sharper relief than in this telling tale related by Sir John.

"He once happened to talk to me about his cousin, Lord Willingdon. 'My cousin, Nigs, he knew a thing or two,' he said. 'An aunt left us both some money and he put his share in that dress shop'. The 'dress shop' was, I think, Molyneux, which of course did very well. I asked Lord De La Warr what he did with his share of the money. He blushed and said 'as a matter of fact I gave it away'. I asked him about this and he said that in the 1914 war he had served in a minesweeper and very much admired the captain. The captain fell on bad times so Lord De La Warr gave him the money."

In 1966, Buck's devoted wife, Diana, died. Two years later, he remarried, this time Sylvia, Countess Kilmuir, the widow of the first and last Earl Kilmuir, a former Lord Chancellor in the Conservative Government. She was the sister of the actor Rex Harrison. She had also, according to family sources, been having an affair with the ninth Earl for some years.

The Earl's later years were spent happily tending the farms in Sussex and indulging his other passion for art – he owned a Bonnard and works by Paul Maze, the French painter who taught Winston Churchill. His love of riding meant he could frequently be seen either on horseback around the estate or busy with a shovel tending to the ditches alongside the rides to ensure they were well-drained.

Fortunately, ill health appears to have escaped him. He died suddenly, on the pavement outside St James' Palace, while on his way to an evening at the theatre, in January 1976, and was buried a few days later in the Sackville family chapel at Withyham parish church.

The ninth Earl had served under four Prime Ministers. He had been one of the last surviving National Labour party politicians to have supported Ramsay MacDonald in 1931. The newspapers all agreed: it was the end of an era.

Cooden Beach Golf Club, 1934. Left to right: Earl De La Warr, Ramsay MacDonald, Lady Kitty, Miss Gampany, Countess De La Warr

Safeguarding the future

The De La Warr family's lands and estate remain extensive even to this day, although the tenth Earl sold the 6,400-acre Ashdown Forest to East Sussex County Council to meet inheritance taxes and keep the forest intact.

The ninth Earl's daughter, now Lady Kitty Giles, still lives near her family home at Fishersgate. A magistrate for over thirty years and on the National Parole Board for five, she works as a member of the Board of Visitors at Brixton Prison and has done so for over twenty years. At the ninth Earl's funeral in Withyham church his grandson, the present Earl, and his son-in-law, Frank Giles, read the lessons.

While the ninth Earl let out the family house at Buckhurst Park, it became a home again for the tenth Earl and today, the eleventh Earl and their families. The oldest part of the house dates back to 1603. Largely rebuilt in 1830 by the fifth Earl De La Warr, it adjoins a large lake fed by the two streams of the Medway and has beautiful views over Ashdown Forest.[20]

The tenth Earl, like his father, was loved and respected in Sussex. In Withyham he built almshouses for local people and at Sackville College, East Grinstead he modernised almshouses which had been built using materials from Old Buckhurst. Besides a business career Lord De La Warr was committed to public service working with the Territorials and the Sussex Youth Association.

The eleventh Earl, who works in the City, maintains both the spirit and fabric of his grandfather's dream in his role as patron of the Pavilion Trust continuing the family's links with Bexhill.

The Pavilion Trust has worked tirelessly to put the Bexhill Pavilion in its rightful place as one of the finest examples of modernist architecture open to the public anywhere in the world today. It has raised extensive funds for the building's sensitive restoration and has continued to champion the concepts on which the building was first founded – identified so eloquently by its originator, Buck De La Warr.

Controversial, pioneering, unconventional and yet graced with a character admired by any who come into contact with it: a description of the De La Warr Pavilion which could as easily apply to the ninth Earl who helped to build it.

Though his life may be over, the influence of the ninth Earl De La Warr – his vision and achievements – is still felt today, in fields as diverse as agriculture, television, politics and, of course, town planning.

Like its founder, the De La Warr Pavilion also continues to influence. As an example of modernist architecture its position is rarely rivalled. Architects the world over now visit Bexhill, as pilgrims would a cathedral, and millions of the general public for whom the Pavilion was designed have walked through its doors.

It was to the ordinary man and woman that the pioneering Earl dedicated both his life, and Bexhill's Pavilion, and in them that he placed his ultimate trust in safeguarding the future. Whatever that future may hold, of both Buck De La Warr and the Pavilion he helped to build and so clearly loved, it can happily be said, each now shares their place in history.

References

1 'Thomas Jefferson Papers: Virginia Records Time Line 1610-1619'. http://lcweb2.loc.gov/ammem/mtjhtml/mtjvatm3.html
2 *A History of the American People to the Civil War*. James Truslow Adams, 1993
3 'Muriel De La Warr'. http://www.spartacus.schoolnet.co.uk/warr.html
4 *Looking Backwards – And Forwards*. George Lansbury, 1935
5 *Candles in the Sun*. Lady Emily Lutyens, 1957
6 *Vita and Harold*. Edited by Nigel Nicholson
7 'Britain in the Thirties'. Ed. Gavin Stamp. *Architectural Design*, Vol.49 No.10–11, 1979
8 Bexhill Museum Association, May 2000
9 'Earl De La Warr and the competition for the Bexhill Pavilion 1933-34'. Russell Stevens and Peter Willis. *Journal of the Society of Architectural Historians of Great Britain*, Vol 33, 1990.
10 *Erich Mendelsohn 1887-1953*. Ed. by Jeremy Brook et al. Modern British Architecture/A3 Times, 1987.
11 *Britain in the Thirties*. Vol 49. Stephen Bayley et al. 1979
12 *Harold Nicholson*. Diaries and Letters.
13 *English History 1914-1945*. A J P Taylor. Oxford.
14 The Pilgrim Trust. 1930–1980
15 *The first ten years: 11th annual report of the Arts Council of Great Britain, 1955-1956*. Arts Council.
16 Obit. *Daily Telegraph*, 29/1/1976
17 'Report of Lord De La Warr's mission to Ethiopia', 1944. East Sussex County Records.
18 *White Mischief*. James Fox. Jonathan Cape, 1982.
19 *Recollections of the Mendelsohn and Chermayeff Practice*. Birkin Haward, 1998
20 *Forest Camera*. Peter Kirby, 1998